MILITARY
INSIGNIA

The new compact study guide and identifier

MILITARY INSIGNIA

The new compact study guide and identifier

William Fowler

CHARTWELL
BOOKS, INC.

A QUINTET BOOK

Published by Chartwell Books
A Division of Book Sales, Inc.
110 Enterprise Avenue
Secaucus, New Jersey 07094

This edition produced for sale
in the U.S.A., its territories
and dependencies only.

ISBN 1–55521–843–1

This book was designed and produced by
Quintet Publishing Limited
6 Blundell Street
London N7 9BH

Creative Director: Richard Dewing
Designer: Stuart Walden
Project Editor: Katie Preston
Editor: Robert Stewart

Typeset in Great Britain by
Central Southern Typesetters, Eastbourne
Manufactured in Singapore by
Eray Scan Pte Ltd
Printed in Singapore by
Star Standard Industries Pte Ltd

Dedication:
Richard and Susan Webster and the staff of
W.S. Supplies, Oxford

CONTENTS

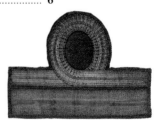

INTRODUCTION

Military insignia, or signs and symbols by which soldiers may be identified, are probably nearly as old as warfare itself. But the origins of modern sophisticated and complex insignia really began with the development of feudalism in the early middle ages. At the heart of the feudal system was the feudal "host", the retinue of armoured knights which every great landowner was compelled to raise and offer, when required, to the king's service. In fact, the knights as often saw action on the battlefield in local warring between rival magnates, and for that purpose each lord's

private army needed to be clearly distinguished by its uniform, or livery, in order to keep knights on the same side from attacking each other. The chief features of feudal liveries were bright colours, easily visible in the hurly-burly of battle, and the great lords' coats of arms.

By the 17th century the functions of uniforms and insignia were becoming more specific and varied. Different symbols and specialist weapons appeared to mark and signify – hence the term, *insignia* – the separate roles of different kinds of soldiers. Musketeers wore distinctive bandoliers; grenadiers had their grenades and slow-

burning matches; the cavalry wore specially designed riding habits. In time, the weapons that soldiers used – for example, the cavalryman's sabre – became incorporated in designs for badges and patches. So military insignia, even of the modern day, carry telltale signs of the history of warfare.

Modern insignia fulfil three functions: they denote the rank and station of a soldier, airman or sailor; they are used to indicate a man's special trade – as, for example, do the wings of a pilot, the anchor cap badge of a sailor and the crossed flags of a signalman; and, perhaps most obvious and important, they signify a man's membership of, and loyalty to, a country, branch of the armed services and regiment.

Ever since the 19th century, when the conscripting of mass national armies be-came a feature of European societies, uniforms and insignia have been standardized. The stripes or chevrons of non-commissioned officers (NCOs), still worn today, date from the Napoleonic wars;

A man becomes the creation of his uniform.

Napoleon I, *Maxims* (1804–15)

---

officers were recognizable by their epaulettes and sashes. From that time, too, dates the practice of giving each regiment its own colours. Regimental colours not only make it easy for a regiment to stick together under the pressure of assault, but they help to instil a sense of group loyalty and camaraderie among the men of each regiment.

FAR LEFT US Army tropical jacket showing the Combat Infantryman's Badge and parachute wings.

LEFT British WWII regimental cloth shoulder titles.

BELOW US Marines during peace-keeping operations in Lebanon.

Insignia give a man or woman in the armed forces a heightened sense of his or her worth and status. They also reinforce the feeling that he or she is part of a team with a collective purpose that transcends individual goals and desires. The use of insignia and colours, of highly distinctive and impressive military uniforms and decorations, to foster undeviating loyalty and patriotism in the armed forces, was

---

This death's livery, which walled its bearers from ordinary life, was a sign they had sold their wills and bodies to the State.

T. E. Lawrence, *The Seven Pillars of Wisdom* (1926)

---

taken to its extreme by the totalitarian states of the 20th century, especially by the Red Army of Stalin's Russia and, even more flamboyantly, by the Nazi rulers of Germany. (Curiously, the designs and insignia of the Nazi armed forces have been retained, in modified form, by modern Germany.)

Camouflage in uniforms was introduced by the British army in India in the mid-19th century, when the traditional white uniforms, so easy for snipers to target, were replaced by khaki (the Urdu word for "dust-coloured"). The US forces continued to wear blue uniforms as late as the Spanish-American war of 1898. The trench warfare of World War I saw the introduction of more elaborate camouflage in the

form of the design now so familiar (and even more essential in modern guerrilla warfare) of splotched leaf-like colours of green, yellow and brown.

As camouflage has become more and more important, insignia have become smaller and more discreet. They are often

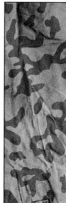

ABOVE Three German camouflage patterns:
1 Rain 2 Quarter shelter 3 Leaf

only to be seen in their full splendour, not on the battlefield, but at ceremonial occasions, when they add to the pageantry of the event. On the other hand, the increasingly specialized nature of modern warfare has meant that more and more insignia have had to be designed to differentiate between the large number of different roles played by modern servicemen and servicewomen. It is no accident that this pocket identifier has many examples of insignia from World War II, for that war, with its huge numbers of enlisted personnel, produced a flowering of badges and insignia.

COLLECTING MILITARY INSIGNIA

An interest in military insignia need not be the preserve of the collector and enthusiast. Forgotten uniforms in closets and cupboards, jackets and overalls bought as work wear, often still have their original badges. Natural interest or curiosity may prompt grandchildren or workmen to wonder what the badges mean.

Badges and insignia also appear in charity shops and car boot sales. Very often the true value of these objects is not known by the people who are selling them. Badges may be mixed up in a mass of brooches and other metal trinkets. Shirts, jackets and tunics with rank and unit insignia may be mixed up with ordinary civilian clothes. For the dedicated collector the discovery of genuine pieces of insignia at good prices can be enormously rewarding.

Shops and specialized markets sell insignia which range from widely issued badges to rare and very costly items, which can command prices in six figures.

As can be imagined where prices are high there is scope for fakes and deception. There are specialized reference works to enable the collector to spot fakes but there is of course the problem that the forger can use these references to ensure that his

BELOW LEFT German 1914–18 General Service Medal.

BELOW British 4th Armoured Brigade flash (Gulf War).

BELOW A shirt showing Master Sergeant's stripes and a US 3rd Army patch.

fake is almost undetectable. One of the simplest ways of identifying a fake or real item of insignia, medal or uniform is to check on its provenance. In some militaria markets there are well-known fakes that have been passed between innocent collectors, but if the item is rare and valuable it is a fair bet that people will want to know how it came on the market. If its origins are suspect it will merely become a curiosity and will not attract big prices.

Faked British title.

Some items, like regimental flags, are so expensive to fake, and so rare, that there is no sense in making a fake. The difficult areas are rare badges – both metal and embroidered cloth. The metal may be made from the original dies and hard to detect from older originals. The cloth can easily be faked and aged.

In markets and auction houses the reputation of the auctioneer and dealers is one guarantee of authenticity. However, even experts can be fooled.

For the collector who finds a rare badge, the question to ask is "In normal circumstances would this badge be on sale?" If the badge is one that was worn by two hundred men two centuries ago, the chances are that it is a fake. The unique and rare do not normally appear on stalls in markets – they sell in auction houses. The rare and uncommon do sometimes appear on uniforms hanging on the clothing rails of charity shops.

The Nazi badges and medals collected by Allied soldiers at the end of World War II were merely attractive items of legitimate "loot". Some are now very valuable, and it may be that the things grandfather brought back from "the War", are worth a substantial sum.

Medals, with their supporting documents and citations can be very valuable. It seems rather sad however that bravery or honourable service, recognized by medals and decorations can become the thing of commercial traffic.

Gallantry awards with their supporting citation do come up for sale, but are normally bought by dealers at high prices.

A good- quality faked WWII Airborne Forces flash.

Vietnam Service Medal awarded between July 4 1965 and March 28 1973.

The medals that are more widely available are campaign decorations which were awarded in very large numbers during the World Wars and subsequent campaigns like Korea, Vietnam and the British and French colonial wars in the 1950s and 60s.

Collectors must beware of unscrupulous traders who combine medals together to produce a bogus set. The inexperienced shopper may be beguiled by what appears to be the medals of a man who either served for a long time, or in theatres across

– FAKING US PATCHES –

The great popularity of military badges has led to the fake manufacture of them throughout the world. Detecting a fake from the real thing can be difficult for the collector. One of the first rules is that the rarer the issue of the badge, the more likely that its appearance on the market is a fake. Finding threads or needle-holes in a badge ripped from a shirt may indicate that the badge is an original, as may a bleached or faded appearance, but marks of wear-and-tear are far from a guarantee of authenticity. The badge may have been deliberately "distressed". Experts can often tell badly made fakes by the use of coloured cloth instead of woven threads, or by stitching that shows that they were not made on the original machines. Most people who like badges, however, do not worry about fakes, because they are now made so well – especially in Asian countries like Japan, Taiwan, Pakistan – that they look attractive and "real" and can command good prices.

RIGHT An informal patch to show the rivalry between the 82nd Airborne Division and the 101st Airborne Division.

the world. Again it is hard to detect a good fake, but the new collector must ask himself or herself whether a soldier could really have lived and fought this long or whether that unit could have been deployed so widely.

Like other military insignia, medals can turn up in unlikely places – charity markets, junk shops and of course among the possessions of deceased relatives or friends.

Some firms will mount the medals and ribbons with a photograph of the recipient, which can be a pleasing way of remembering the service of friends or relations.

Collecting militaria, medals and insignia can for some people become an addiction. They will follow a regiment, campaign or even an individual and build up a wealth of material. This can involve considerable sacrifice and heartache when they find that the last bits of a collection are rare and consequently expensive. Ironically these items need not be exotic. Collectors of World War I uniforms normally have a problem finding authentic boots, shirts and socks – all of these continued to be used after 1918 and so were worn out. Fine parade quality uniforms and insignia normally survive.

With these caveats in mind, collecting military insignia can be a fascinating insight into national and military history. It can be an inexpensive hobby if the collector is sensible and, with recent wars like Vietnam and the Gulf as sources for material, it is an area where new collectors start with the same advantages and disadvantages as those who are experienced.

BELOW A group of Italian fascists wearing the party uniform at a village fair, near Trieste.

IDENTIFIER

This book will help collectors of military insignia to identify items that they find in shops and markets, especially when individual pieces – a badge or a patch – are found in isolation from their original uniform. It is also meant to assist people who see pictures in the newspapers and on television of soldiers and paramilitary forces in conflicts around the world. It is worth remembering, in using this guide, that armed forces consist of three groups – officers, non-commissioned officers or NCOs, and other ranks (enlisted men in the US services). They are organized into groups, or teams, of varying sizes, from the relatively small platoons, through large divisions, to the full-scale, many thousand strong, naval task force or army group.

The entries in this identifier have been divided into two main sections. In the first section the entries have been arranged, as far as is possible, according to the place where insignia are to be found on the body, starting with cap badges and moving downwards. Almost without exception insigna and distinctive uniform markings have, throughout history, been confined to the upper body above the waist. The second section, SYMBOLS AND HERALDRY, has entries on the motifs most often seen in military insignia, for example swords, axes etc.

Rank, qualification and organization insignia appear on various areas of a serviceman's uniform. For quick identification of where they are located the following symbols have been employed:–

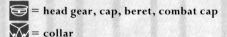 = head gear, cap, beret, combat cap

= collar

= breast, normally above the belt and on or near the top pockets

= shoulder

= upper arm

= mid arm

= cuff

CAP BADGES

A cap badge – perhaps the most immediately arresting of all military insignia and the focus of any uniform – is worn on a beret, a service-dress peaked cap, side hat and a combat cap. It may also be painted on a helmet. In a few armies beret badges and forage cap badges are sometimes worn on the collar or shoulder straps. Cap badges are traditionally made of brass or white metal, but in modern times they are also made of non-polish materials. Cap badges may identify the nationality of a soldier by displaying the national emblem; but they also, more modestly, simply identify the wearer's branch of the armed services or his regiment. Some armies make use of cap badges to distinguish between officers, NCOs and the ranks, officers being given a metal-thread badge, the others a metal badge.

1

2

3

4

1 Imperial Austria-Hungary cap badge for officer's dress shako.

2 British naval officer's cap badge (c. 1910).

3 US Army officer's peaked cap badge.

4 US Army enlisted man's peaked cap badge.

REGIMENTAL BADGES

The British, Commonwealth and former Imperial forces favour corps or regimental cap badges. In infantry and cavalry regiments these can be very elaborate with historical designs and associations. The Gurkha regiments in the British army have badges with crossed kukris. Australian Army badges feature such non-heraldic animals as the swan and kangaroo. French beret badges are normally an open metal circle which encloses a symbolic design like hunting horns or winged wheels; the exception is the badge of the Marine Commandos formed during World War II, which has a shield shape and shows the Cross of Lorraine, a sailing ketch and a Fairburn Sykes dagger. The Edelweiss mountain flower has been favoured for mountain troops in European armies.

1 Cap badge of the 5th Royal Gurkha Rifles (Frontier Force).

2 18th Australian Light Horse (Western Australia Mounted Infantry).

3 12th Australian Light Horse (New England Light Horse).

4 German mountain troops' "edelweiss".

5 French Marine Commando beret badge.

6 Beret badge of the French Infantry.

NATIONAL CAP BADGES

A national cap badge is often a form of national insignia (qv). The Norwegian Army has both metal and cloth badges with the cypher OV, for King Olav V. The former Soviet Union favoured the red star with a hammer and sickle in the middle, though undemocratically it had a different badge for officers. Interestingly, troops of the Imperial Japanese Army in World War II also wore a red star as their cap badge. Before the collapse of Communism, the red star appeared in the cap badges of many of the Warsaw Pact armies, though in the case of the Hungarians it was set against the national colours.

1 Norwegian beret badge with cypher of King Olaf V.

2 1922 Red Army cap badge.

3 1955 Soviet Army officer's cap badge.

4 Modern Soviet Army cap badge for dress uniform.

5 Hungarian army officer's cap badge.

SWEETHEART BADGES

Miniature copies of cap badges were struck in silver in World War I and worn by wives and sweethearts of soldiers serving at the front. Some used a military button (qv) in lieu of the cap badge. Mother-of-pearl as well as a gold wash on silver enhanced their appearance. Enamel work added colour. By World War II RAF wings and Royal Navy insignia were popular. Since the War these badges have become more elaborate and more a type of jewellery. Materials can include gold and precious stones and as a result the cost has put them out of the reach of ordinary soldiers.

1

2

3

4

Five British regimental sweetheart badges:

1 London Rifle Brigade.
2 Queen Victoria's Rifles.
3 Queen's Westminsters.
4 Civil Service Rifles.
5 Tower Hamlets Rifles.

5

BERETS

Symbolic colours have been adopted for berets. The United Nations forces wear pale blue. Maroon is commonly worn by airborne forces, though the former Soviet Union favoured pale blue. Naval personnel wear dark blue. Light infantry in European armies wear dark green, though this is the colour of US Special Forces, who have a series of shield-shaped coloured backings to their badge. Soviet Naval Infantry wear dark blue, while Royal Marines in the United Kingdom wear green. Khaki brown, sometimes with a coloured backing for the cap badge, is worn by some British regiments, including the Guards. The Netherlands adopted regimental and branch-of-service badges for berets in 1950. In France the Chasseurs Alpine wear a large dark blue beret, which in World War I was the original military beret.

1 Riggers from the US 82nd Airborne wearing the trademark red beret of airborne soldiers.

2 Dutch post World War II beret badges depicting branch of service by backing and badge:

a Signals.

b Supply Corps.

c Medical Corps.

COCKADES

The cockade is a circular or oval multi-coloured disc which is part of a cap badge and which shows national or regional colours. In the Imperial German Army in World War I cockades were elaborate and showed the principalities and areas of Germany from which the regiments were recruited. In World War II a cockade of red, black and white was combined with the Reichsadler, the Nazi swastika and eagle. The modern Belgian army has a red, yellow and black, the German army a yellow, red and black and the Norwegians a blue, white and red cockade.

1

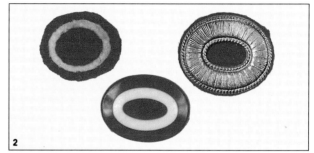

2

4

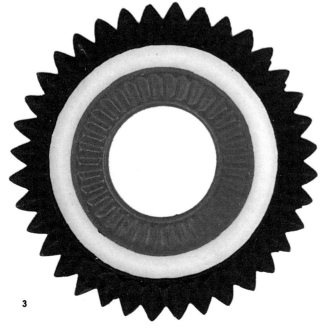

3

1 Belgian cap badge.

2 Three Danish cockades.

3 National cockade from the Empire of Germany worn on *pickelhaube* helmet.

4 Prussian state cockade from the German empire for the *pickelhaube.*

BOSSES

A boss is a coloured circular backing which stands proud of a cap or beret and is worn by British Rifle, Light Infantry and Gurkha regiments. Like a conventional cap

badge backing the colour of the boss has regimental significance – for example dark green for Rifle Regiments, red for Gurkha and black for Light Infantry.

1

2

1 1st George's V's Own Gurkha Rifles cap badge on red boss.

2 5th Royal Gurkha Rifles cap badge on black boss.

3 British boss usually worn with regimental badge fixed in the centre.

3

CAP TALLIES

The black ribbon cap band on naval ratings' caps frequently showed the name of the ship, though during World War II this was discontinued for reasons of security. In post-war navies the former East German Navy retained the practice, with their ratings wearing a tally reading Volksmarine. The Royal Danish Navy has a tally which reads KGL MARINE with a coloured ribbon rosette on the side.

1 Cap tally for the LSD HMS Fearless which served in the Falklands War in 1982.

1

HACKLES

Fusilier and certain highland infantry regiments in the British Army have a hackle as part of their cap badge. This is a bundle of feathers behind the badge and in its original form had regimental significance – the Lancashire Fusiliers had yellow, the Royal Irish green, Royal Iniskilling grey, and the Royal Northumberland white with a red top. This two-colour design has been adopted for the amalgamated regiments which now make up the Royal Regiment of Fusiliers.

Polish and Italian mountain troops have soft felt mountaineers' caps with feathers.

1 Hackle of the Black Watch (The Royal Highland Regiment).

2 Two British army sergeants in the 1950's.

1

CHINSTRAPS

As the name suggests, the chinstrap was originally intended to secure a cap or helmet, which was particularly important for cavalry soldiers. It has now become largely symbolic and is worn on service dress caps, secured with two small buttons with regimental or national insignia. Some armies, like the German, distinguish between NCOs, who have a plain leather chinstrap, and officers, who have a gilt cord strap. The distinction between chinstraps can also be enhanced by coloured or woven cap bands for senior, middle-rank and non-commissioned officers.

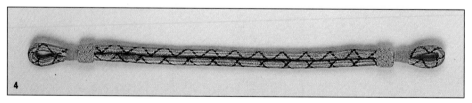

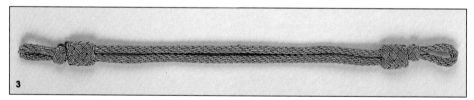

1 British Army officer's chinstrap.

2 Italian Brigadier General's chinstrap.

3 "Nationale Volksarmee" officer's chinstrap.

4 Yugoslav chinstrap.

DISTINCTION LACE

Distinction lace consists of strips of gold or silver woven cloth of varying widths and patterns. It is now used primarily as rank insignia but has been used to trim uniforms, including peaked caps where it is sometimes known as "scrambled egg", and in the making of sword knots (qv). Distinction lace can also be used as an edging to collars to indicate rank, for example by the Polish, Austrian and Norwegian armies. It is used on shoulder straps where it is again a rank indicator, for example in the Royal Navy. Bands of lace around the cuffs also indicate rank in Royal Navy and Royal Air Force officers. Until 1948, Italian army officers wore a combination of stripes – wide and narrow stripes for field officers and narrow stripes only for company officers – on both their peaked caps and on the sleeves beneath the curl.

1

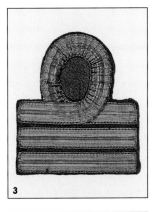

3

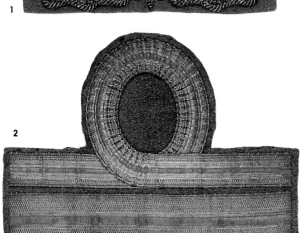

2

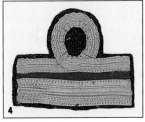

4

1 Italian army rank insignia worn on the forearm:

a Brigadier.

b Major.

c Captain.

d Major, Medical Corps.

COLLAR INSIGNIA

Before the 20th century the method used by most armies to identify a soldier's branch of the armed services was to give the uniform of each branch a distinctive collar colour. It then became the custom to use collar insignia, both patches and badges, for the purpose – chiefly, no doubt, because by having collars all the same colour, uniforms could be mass produced in one design. The collar may be open like the lapels of a conventional jacket. Open fronted collars can be used to display up to four items of insignia. The US armed forces display both rank on the collars of working, shirt sleeve and combat dress and the letters "US" on service dress lapels. Officers show the insignia of their arm on the lapels. Stand and fall collars, which button to the neck, like those worn by many European armies in the two World Wars, could have designs which showed rank and arm by a combination of coloured piping, badges and distinction lace (qv).

1a

2

3

1b

1 Austrian collar patches indicating rank by the combination of distinction lace and stars:

a Senior NCO.

b Junior NCO.

2 Bronze collar badge of US Army officer.

3 Bronze collar badge of US Army enlisted man.

COLLAR DOGS

These are small metal badges, which were backed by a split pin, but are now more commonly backed by a clutch pin. In the former USSR collar dogs are screw backed. In the British Army collar dogs can be smaller versions of the regimental or corps cap badge. They appear on khaki service dress and also on the lapels of mess kit worn by officers and senior NCOs. Like cap badges they are often representative. For example, some Warsaw Pact armies had collar dogs with tanks for armoured troops, or a hammer and wrench for logistic troops.

1a

2a

2b

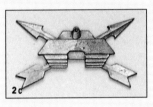

2c

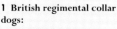

1b

2d

2e

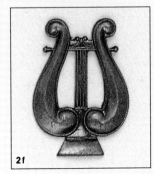

2f

2 Collar dogs of the Federal Republic of Germany's Bundeswehr:

a Artillery.

b Signals.

c Panzerjäger.

d Engineers.

e Medical.

f Band.

1 British regimental collar dogs:

a The King's Regiment (Liverpool).

b The Royal Dragoons.

COLLAR PATCHES

These are normally made of felt and have rank (qv), regiment and arm insignia attached. Between the wars a number of European armies, including the early Red Army, favoured the French style, which was triangular and attached to the tips of the collar. Probably the most elaborate were the German Army and Air Force (Luftwaffe) patches, which were in arm colours. Some colours, like red for artillery or flak artillery, were common to both forces. Luftwaffe ranks were displayed on the collar by a combination of wings and wreaths. Army ranks were shown by piping and lace, which were also repeated in coloured piping on shoulder straps (qv).

1a

1 Democratic Republic of Germany ("Nationale Volksarmee") collar patches:

a Army general.

b Air Force general.

2 French 129th Infantry Regiment collar patch.

3 Turkish Army collar patches:

a Doctor.

b Armour.

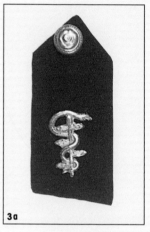

3a

1b

2

3b

GORGETS

This combination of a coloured collar patch, with a button and either gold lace oak leaf motif or silk cord, is worn by officers above the rank of Lieutenant-Colonel or equivalent. In some countries the distinction is worn by Air Force as well as Army officers. White gorgets are worn by Royal Navy midshipmen and officer cadets at the Royal Military Academy, Sandhurst. The name gorget dates back to the metal neck protection worn by officers in the late 18th and early 19th centuries. The Germans continued this tradition with a metal gorget on a chain which was worn by standard bearers on parades and, more notably, by the Feldgendarmerie, the Military police when they were on duty.

1 British gorget patches worn at the front of a stand collar:

a General.

b Brigadier and substantive colonel.

c As b but small size.

d As b but of the Royal Army Medical Corps.

IDENTITY TAGS

1

While strictly not a part of military insignia, a soldier's identity tags – commonly known as dog tags – are normally hung on a chain around a soldier's neck. They normally consist of two tags one of which can be left with the soldier if he is killed and the other returned to his unit. The tag carries information like name, blood group, date of birth and religion. The first identity tags were sewn onto uniforms in the 19th century and this tradition is perpetuated by the name tags that many armies have on combat uniforms. The information displayed above the tunic pockets of US uniforms says either US Navy, USMC, US Army or US Air Force. On the other side is the owner's name.

2

1 **British Army.**
2 **Austro-Hungarian Army.**
3 **US Army.**

SHOULDER STRAPS

Shoulder straps can show rank with stars and other motifs; arm and corps are normally identified by coloured backings or pipings. They can be attached to the shoulder of a uniform jacket or tunic and have an open buttoned end at the neck which allows the cross straps from load-carrying equipment to be slipped underneath. Shoulder straps are normally unstiffened or only semi stiffened. On dress uniforms a stiffened shoulder board can be removed because it is attached with a button-and-loop fixture. Stiffened boards were favoured by former Warsaw Pact armies and the Soviet Union.

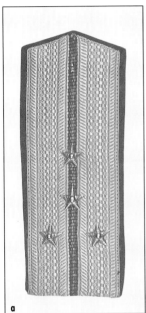

a

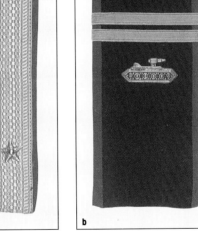

b

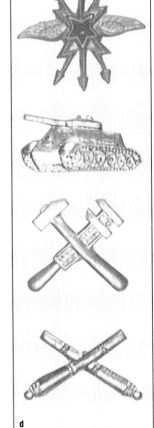

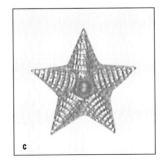

c

d

1 Soviet shoulder boards:

a Captain, Infantry.

b Junior Sergeant, Armour.

c Field officer's star.

d Group of four modern branch of service badges for Soviet shoulder boards.

EPAULETTES

The word epaulette is derived from the French *épaule* – shoulder – and strictly consists of a shoulder board with tasselled fringe. Originally epaulettes were bundles of cords attached to the shoulder of uniforms to prevent shoulder belts from slipping off. They became fashionable in the Napoleonic era and today are still worn as part of full dress uniforms and by bandsmen. On parade French Foreign Legionnaires wear striking red and green epaulettes.

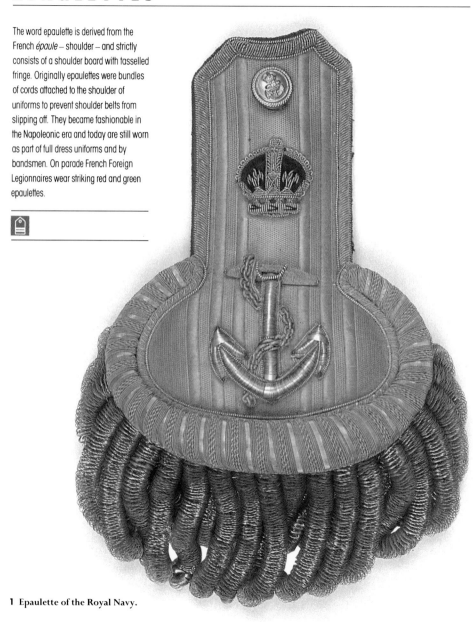

1 Epaulette of the Royal Navy.

ARM COLOURS

These can appear as the backing to rank on collars or shoulder straps, as piping or as coloured bars incorporated into rank insignia. In parade uniforms or mess kit, arm colours may appear as broad stripes on the outside seams of trousers. Historically this is the origin of the pejorative term "leg" used by US airborne forces for non-airborne troops. "Red Leg" was the name for artillerymen in the Civil War because of the red stripe on their trousers. In the inter-war period, as the US Army experimented with armoured formations, it produced a triangular patch (qv) with the yellow of the cavalry, red of artillery and blue of infantry and a track design in the centre. Though national armies have adopted their own arm or unit colours, medical services seem to favour purple as an arm colour and the staff of Aesculapius as a cap or collar badge.

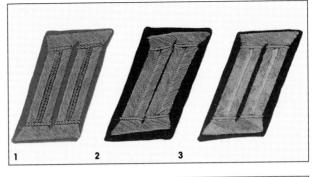

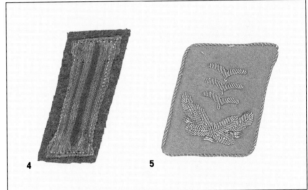

Third Reich collar patches:

1 Army Recruiting Service/ Field Police.

2 Anti-Tank.

3 Signals.

4 Rank and file tattoo World War II pattern.

5 Air Force Flying Personnel/ Parachutists.

6 Medical officer.

7 Anti-Aircraft.

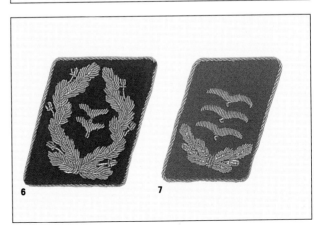

RANK BADGES

Rank is conventionally displayed on the shoulders, upper arm and cuff – officers' rank on shoulder straps (qv), non-commissioned officers' (NCOs) with chevrons (qv) on the upper arm and senior NCOs on the cuff. Some Naval and Air Force officers display rank on their cuffs. In World War I the British Army discontinued the practice of officers wearing rank on the cuff because it made them obvious targets for snipers. For simplicity, when personnel are in working rig, combat kit or pullover order, shoulder straps can be used by all ranks. Under these conditions the insignia are normally attached to a slip-on or slide (qv), which can be removed for security reasons. The French pioneered the practice of displaying rank on the upper breast, which, unlike the shoulder, is uncluttered by webbing and load-carrying equipment. The US armed forces use stars (qv), eagles (qv), leaves and bars (qv), all worn on shoulder straps, to indicate the rank of officers.

1a

1b

1 **World War II German shoulder cords indicating rank:**

a **Armeegeneral.**

b **Colonel, Air Force.**

2 **Major of the US Army.**

3 **Colonel of the US Army.**

2

3

BARS

In some armed forces officers' ranks are displayed by a series of silver or gold bars attached to the shoulder strap or cap. In the US Army a 2nd Lieutenant has a gold bar, which produces the nickname "Butter Bar". Lieutenants have a silver bar and

Captains two silver bars. Rank can be worn on the shoulder or on a cap or beret. The French armed forces have a system of bars which rise from senior NCO, through Officer Candidate, to the five bars which indicate that the officer is a Colonel. Naval

and Air Force rank can be displayed on shoulder straps as bars which conform to those worn on the cuff of a jacket.

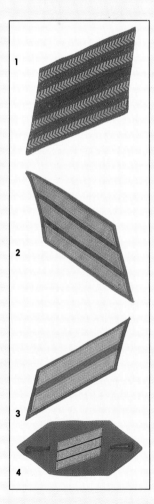

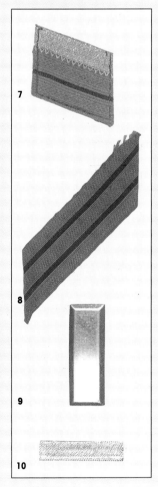

1 Belgian First Sergeant.

2 Hauptgefreiter of the Federal Republic of Germany's Army (Bundeswehr).

3 Obergefreiter of the Bundeswehr.

4 French Sergent Chef.

5 Captain of the US Army.

6 2nd Lieutenant of the US Army.

7 French "Brigadier Chef" of the Hussars.

8 Rank insignia of "Cabo" of Spanish Air Force.

9 Metal bar of American 1st Lieutenants.

10 Narrow bar worn on collar patches by Belgian field officers.

STARS

Stars are a way to display rank from Second Lieutenant to Captain. While some are identifiable as stars, with between four and eight points, others are diamond-shaped metal fittings. Conventionally, a Second Lieutenant has one star, a Lieutenant two and a Captain three. In armies with a monarch as head of state, stars reappear between the ranks of Colonel and Major General and finally as a General's rank. On combat clothing and shirt-sleeve order, officers wear slip-ons (qv) with either stars or "pips" embroidered; some have coloured felt backings to indicate the arm or corps of the wearer. Stars are normally worn on shoulder straps, but may be displayed on loops on the front of combat jackets.

Officers in the Spanish Marines and Air Force display stars on their cuffs. In the US armed forces stars are worn by officers from the rank of Brigadier General upwards.

a

b

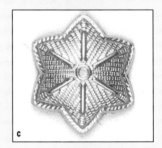

c

d

e

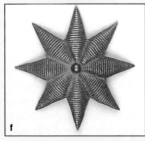

f

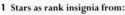

1 Stars as rank insignia from:
a Belgium.
b Britain.
c Denmark, for field officers.
d Germany.
e Italy.
f Spain.
2 Belgian Colonel of Infantry.

2

SWORDS

Two crossed swords or sabres, or one crossed with a military baton, have long been used as insignia for Generals in the British and Commonwealth armies. Combined with a star (qv) or crown (qv), or both, they distinguish the rank of Major

General (a two-star post) through Lieutenant-General to General. Rank (four-star) may be displayed on collars, shoulder straps or the cap. Among NATO armed forces, the Greek Army and Navy, the Spanish Army, Marines and Air Force,

and the Turkish Army, Navy and Air Force all have a crossed-sword device for Generals or the equivalent.

1 **Rank insignia of a British Army General.**

2 **Royal crest worn by brigadiers and substantive colonels of the British Army as a cap badge.**

3 **Shoulder strap of a Royal Navy Vice-Admiral.**

3

SLIP-ONS OR SLIDES

A slip-on, or slide, is normally a cloth loop about the same size as the shoulder strap and shows the rank and sometimes the unit or formation of the wearer. The Italian and Israeli armies have slip-ons which include a flap that hangs from the shoulder and displays the soldier's formation.

Officer cadets or candidates for Officer or NCO courses may wear coloured slip-ons to distinguish them from ordinary soldiers. The US Army has a dark green slip-on which identifies the wearer as a combat leader, a soldier who can lead troops in combat in an emergency. Slip-ons may be

made from material which is the same colour or pattern as the shirt or combat kit to which they are attached.

1

2

3

4

5

1 Australian Army Headquarters slip-on.

2 Polish Army slip-on plastic shoulder title and metal formation sign.

3 Italian slip-on displaying title, formation sign and rank insignia.

4 Jordanian Army General.

5 Yugoslav Army First Captain.

FOURRAGERES AND AIGUILLETTES

Fourrageres and aiguillettes are looped from the shoulder, through the epaulette (qv), and attached to the chest or pocket of the officer, NCO or soldier. Aiguillettes are either in silver or gold and normally worn by officers who are aides-de-camp to Generals or monarchs. They are a symbolic representation of the hobbling harness an aid would carry to secure a General's horse when he was in the field. Fourrageres, which are French by origin, are two or three coloured silk cords and can be worn as a regimental or individual distinction. Soldiers may wear more than one if in the past their unit has distinguished itself in action several times.

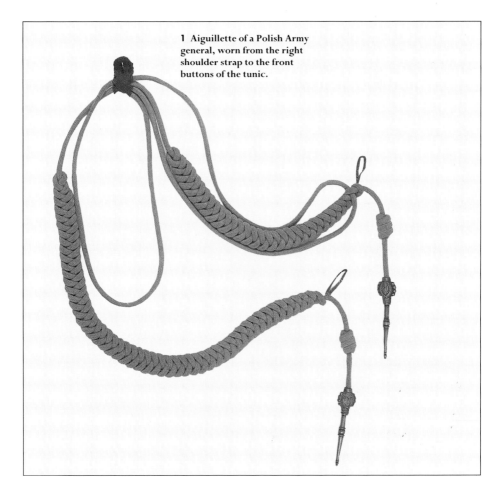

1 Aiguillette of a Polish Army general, worn from the right shoulder strap to the front buttons of the tunic.

LANYARDS AND WHISTLE CORDS

Lanyards and whistle cords can be in one or two colours and are worn by officers or NCOs. While originally intended to secure a whistle they are now largely symbolic. Conventions exist in the British Army as to the side on which they should be worn – officers on the right and NCOs on the left, with Warrant Officers entitled to wear an officer's lanyard. British Royal Marine officers wear a lanyard on each shoulder which show respectively that they are commissioned and with which Commando unit they are serving.

British Army lanyards and whistlecords:

1 Royal Artillery NCO's lanyard.

2 Royal Engineers NCO's lanyard.

3 Royal Greenjackets officer's whistlecord.

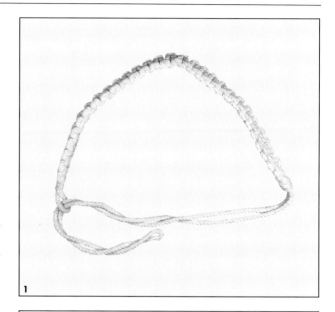

1

2

3

TABS

Shoulder tabs are a curved embroidered badge worn on the shoulder and the most widely known are Airborne and Ranger. A Ranger tab was first worn in World War II. The growth in specialized tabs took place in the Vietnam War, when they were manufactured locally. They included units like Recondo, the 22nd Pathfinder Airborne Detachment, the Wolfhounds, Kit Carson Scout and, rather intriguingly, Combat Artists. The black and gold Ranger Tab is a much sought-after military qualification within the US Army. Other tabs may show ships' names in a way similar to a ship's tally (qv) or operational services like Lebanon or Desert Storm.

1 Recondo, Special Forces and Airborne tabs in full colour and subdued.

2 Ranger tab.

TITLES

A title is similar in many ways to a tab, though it can also be brass or a white or black coloured metal. Metal titles are normally worn on the shoulder strap (qv) and cloth on the shoulder. The title bears the name of the soldier's regiment, organization or nationality. British battle dress between the 1930s and 1950s had titles on coloured felt, often in corps or regimental colours. The Royal Marines retained the title Royal Marine Commando and wore it on their jerseys. The cloth title has recently been re-adopted by some regiments in the British Army with the introduction of the SA80 rifle. During World War II, Commonwealth and Allied forces in occupied Europe – Poland and Canada, for instance – wore national titles. One enterprising Texan, flying with an RAF Eagle Squadron before the United States entered World War II, received permission from King George to wear a title reading "Texas".

1 Gilt and silver shoulder title from The Royal Northumberland Fusiliers.

2 Anodized metal title from The Royal Anglian Regiment.

3 Royal Marine Commando cloth title.

4 Three British regimental cloth titles.

5 Three national titles.

PATCHES

The embroidered felt patch worn on the upper shoulder dates back to simple one-colour designs worn in the American Civil War, but it has now been elevated to almost an art form. In the US Army a soldier wears the patch of the unit with which he is serving on his left shoulder and, if he has previously seen combat, the patch of the unit with which he was serving on the right shoulder. Until the Vietnam War patches were exotic full-colour insignia, but because they detracted from camouflage they were replaced with subdued designs of black thread on olive drab. Full-colour patches are now worn only on dress green or blue uniforms.

1

2

4

3

1 28th Infantry Division.
2 Special Forces (subdued).
3 Infantry School.
4 77th Infantry Division.

ARMY PATCHES

Of the US Army patches possibly the most interesting is that of the 5th Army which landed in Morocco under General Mark W Clark. In 1943 he approved a patch which had the silhouette of a mosque as a backdrop to commemorate this campaign in World War II. The 1st Army has a simple "A" on a white and red backdrop, but this patch has been produced in many variations, including an A with a white, blue, yellow, red and black centre against an olive drab backdrop. The 2nd Army has a figure "2" in red and white on khaki.

2

1

3

1 5th Army patch adopted in 1943. The original patch consisted of five stars.

2 1st Army patch (new). In the 1930s the "A" was on a ground coloured according to branch of service.

3 2nd Army patch.

CORPS PATCHES

Among the US Army Corps' patches the 2nd is interesting since it shows an American eagle (qv) and a British lion (qv) flanking a Roman-numeral figure 2. It commemorates the deployment of the Corps to the United Kingdom in World War II. Seven Corps has a seven-pointed star enclosing a Roman seven. With a sense of fun, 13th Corps had a lucky four-leaf clover as the backdrop to a red triangle. The US Marine Corps 3rd Corps had a dragon (qv) with the numeral III, while the 5th Corps had an alligator with three stars. Both were on a shield design and in traditional USMC red and yellow.

1 2nd Corps patch.

2 13th Corps patch.

3 US Marine Corps Aviation, 3rd Wing.

1

2

3

DIVISION PATCHES

Some of these, like those of the US 1st Infantry Division – "The Big Red One" – and the 1st Cavalry are very striking. Others, like the 5th, 28th, 88th and 91st, are simple blocks of colour dating back to Civil War designs. Many have nicknames. The "TO" cattle-brand design of the 90th Infantry Division stands for Texas and Oklahoma, but its members asserted that it stood for Tough Ombres – Tough Men. Wags in the 101st Airborne said that the "AA" of the 82nd Airborne actually stood for "Almost Airborne" rather than "All American". Some Divisional patches, like that of the 79th, with its Cross of Lorraine,

and the 93rd, with a French helmet, are designs which date back to the American Expeditionary Force of World War I. The National Guard 49th Division has the figure of a gold panner in blue against a red and yellow shield. The Marine Corps

detachment in Londonderry, Northern Ireland, had a USMC badge in yellow on a red shield, with a shamrock.

1 1st Infantry Division patch.

2 90th Infantry Division patch.

3 82nd Airborne Division patch.

4 5th Infantry Division patch.

CAVALRY AND BRIGADE PATCHES

The patches of the US Cavalry keep to the traditional yellow, which was first used in bandanas and piping on uniforms. The 1st Cavalry, also known as the "First Team" or "Hell for Leather", has a yellow shield with an oblique black bar and a horse's head. The 2nd Cavalry has a blue chevron and two stars. A common feature of US Army Brigade patches is the four-sided shape, slightly bulging at top and bottom, although some brigade patches are shields, diamonds and circles. US Army Infantry and Army brigades were raised in

the 1960s and received appropriate patches. Some were exact copies of those of the old World War II divisions which had been disbanded after the war. During the Vietnam War the 173rd Airborne Brigade produced very informal variants of its winged bayonet (qv) patch, one showed a winged pipe with the motto "The Herd" and the other showed a black and white fist interlocked against a backdrop which reads "Two Shades of Soul Togetherness" with "The Herd" at the top of the patch. There are currently five Armoured Divisions

in the US Army – the 1st (Old Ironsides), 2nd (Hell on Wheels), 3rd (Spearhead), 49th (Lone Star) and 50th (Jersey Blues). The latter two are divisions of the Army National Guard. All Armoured Divisions have the triangular patch split into red, yellow and blue – the colours of the cavalry, infantry and artillery – the components of an armoured formation.

1 1st Cavalry Division patch.

2 75th Infantry Brigade (subdued) patch.

3 199th Infantry Brigade patch.

4 2nd Armoured Division patch.

5 67th Infantry Brigade.

SCHOOLS AND CENTRES INSIGNIA

The US Army has a logical approach to insignia for schools and centres. They are triangular and in arm colours (qv) at the centre is the torch of knowledge (which was also the cap badge for the British Royal Army Education Corps). This motif is, in its directness, like the crossed flintlock pistols of the Military Police or the winged (qv) wheel of transportation.

Schools run by units favour more colourful designs. The 2nd Infantry Division Advanced Combat Training Academy (ACTA) based in Korea has a breast badge showing an Indian Head arrow piercing the red North Korea. The US Army Chemical Corps school has crossed chemist's retorts. Crossed retorts against a palm tree were also worn by British 1

Division Chemical Warfare experts during the Gulf War. Officer cadets in the British Army wear white loops on their shoulder straps or white gorgets (qv) on parade uniform.

1

2

3

4

5

1 Transport School patch.
2 Imjin River Scouts pocket badge.
3 Aviation School patch.

4 Signal Corps Centre and School patch.
5 Chemical Warfare Unit 1st (Br) Div. (Gulf War).

FLASHES

In 1990–91 the British public followed the exploits of 4 and 7 Armoured Brigades which together made up 1 (Br) Division in the Gulf. Seven Armoured Brigade wore a flash showing a red jerboa and boasted the name "Desert Rats". Flashes were the name the British and Commonwealth forces gave to their patches. Like the US equivalents they ranged from Army down through Corps, Division and Brigade. Like their US originals designs reflected local geography or history. In World War II the British 1st, 2nd, 8th and 14th armies all had a shield design. The 9th army had an elephant, a pun on the nickname of its commander, General Sir Henry "Jumbo" Wilson. An Assyrian lion was worn by the 10th Army, which was based in Iraq. British Corps drew on animal motifs,

including a fish for the 2nd, an elephant for the 4th, a wild cat for the 9th, a ram for the 13th, a lion for the 25th and a boar for the 30th. The 3rd Army Corps was commanded by Lieutenant-General Sir Ronald Adam and so its flash was a fig leaf. Since the war arm insignia have been adopted by French, German, Italian and Warsaw Pact forces.

2

1 **7th Armoured Brigade (Gulf War).**

2 **French 2nd Army flash, machine embroidered on a felt background in the USA.**

3 **8th Division of the French Army, made of woven silk sewn on a black felt backing.**

4 **Federal Republic of Germany 6th Armoured Division flash.**

SUBMARINE INSIGNIA

The risks and challenges of submarine operations give the insignia awarded to their crews a status akin to army parachute wings. The most widely worn have dolphins either single or as a pair with a national crest at the centre. Italian submariners in World War II had a circular badge with a single dolphin and the word,

"Sommergibili". In World War II US submariners had dolphins flanking a submarine. Since the war semi-official patches (qv) have been produced for individual boats and their operations.

a

1 Two woven badges of the US Navy:

a The nuclear submarine USS "Swordfish".

b The USS "George Washington".

b

SQUADRON BADGES

Originally painted on the nose of aircraft in World War I, squadron badges are now more commonly worn on flying suits by aircrew. For security and ease of cleaning they are backed with hook and pile fabric. They may be worn on the shoulder or the right breast. Some Air Forces, like the British Royal Air Force, have very formally designed badges; other countries have adopted badges which are almost cartoon characters. During World War II a US Marine Bombardment wing had Felix the cat carrying a round bomb with a fizzing fuse.

1 Italian Aerobatic team, Red Devils.

2 366 Fighter Bomber Group, US Air Force, stationed at Aviano.

1

2

AIR FORCE BADGES

Before the United States Army Air Force became a separate force in 1947 it was an arm of the US Army. Its badges featured a white star with a red circular centre and the colours blue and yellow. Unassigned personnel in the USAAF wore a blue circular patch with a yellow winged white star. Designs for the different Air Forces were bold and original, probably the most striking of them being that of the 7th Air Force, which had the figure "7" piercing an oblique star. The 8th Air Force, which bore the brunt of the daylight air war against Germany, had a winged figure "8" enclosing a star.

1 7th Air Force patch.
2 8th Air Force patch.
3 US Army Air Force patch.

PILOT'S WINGS

With rotary-wing aircraft as well as fixed-wing, these wings can include helicopter pilots. They may be in embroidered felt, metal or metal and enamel. Some forces have wings whose designs distinguish between army, navy and air force and between navigator, weapons officer and pilot. In some forces only a pilot has a badge with two wings; other crew have one wing. The conventional design has a central motif, which may be the national or Air Force insignia, flanked by open wings. The central motif may show if the member of the air crew is the pilot, navigator or engineer or it may show the level of experience the pilot has attained.

1 Austrian wings.
2 Royal Air Force air crew single wings.
3 Royal Air Force pilot's double-winged badge.

4 "Luftwaffe" pilot wings.
5 Polish wings worn on the left breast with the hook pinned under the lapel of the jacket.

PARACHUTE WINGS

Parachute wings fall into a class of their own and may be worn on the chest or shoulder. Some, like the Belgian, German and British wings, are in embroidered cloth, while others, like those worn by the French and US Armies, are metal badges. While the ability to make a series of military parachute jumps may be regarded as a trade, the challenge of the jumps and the build-up to them can reasonably be said to put parachute wings in their own class. The design common to most wings consists of a parachute flanked by open eagle's wings. The US Army has different wings for Parachutist, Senior 30 jumps (including 15 with combat equipment), Ranger for Ranger-qualified soldiers and Master 64 jumps (25 with combat equipment, four at night, five mass tactical jumps and "jumpmaster" qualification).

1

2

3

1 **Spanish parachute badge.**

2 **Cambodian wings, basic brevet.**

3 **Ugandan wings, basic brevet.**

4 **US Army parachute senior.**

5 **US Army parachute master.**

6 **British SAS parachute wings.**

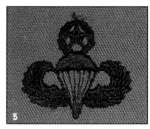

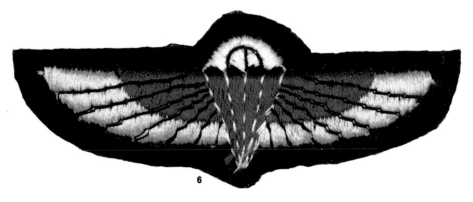

6

PROFICIENCY AND TRADE INSIGNIA

In the Army these badges can, for example, show that a man is a marksman – a skill – or an Assault Pioneer – a trade. The trade and skill badges may be worn on different cuffs, while some armed forces display them as metal or cloth badges worn on the chest. A marksman's skills may be recognized by a lanyard (qv), but often the badges show a symbolic representation, like crossed flags for signallers or the axes (qv) for a pioneer. In the former Soviet Union soldiers were awarded a series of numbered enamel badges as they became more highly qualified. The US armed forces have awarded badges and decorations for peacetime expertise, but also made a distinction with the combat Infantry Badge (qv) for operational performance.

1

2

3

1 British Army trade badge worn by assault pioneers.

2 British skill-at-arms badge for signallers.

3 British skill-at-arms badge for motor mechanics.

4 Hungarian metal trade badges with proficiency number.

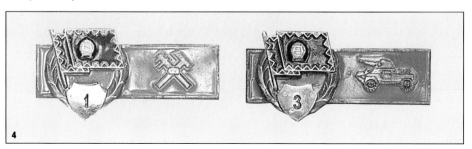

4

SPECIALITY AND DISTINGUISHING MARKS

These badges are the naval equivalent of proficiency and trade insignia. In the British Royal Navy these trade patches are known as non-substantive insignia. As in the US Navy they show graphically the seaman's trade and can include signaller's flags, radar or radio technician or diver. The first non-substantive badge

adopted by the Royal Navy was in 1860 and showed a cannon; the torpedo was adopted in 1903 and C for cook in 1932. In the US Navy a baker cook has a C and steward a C with horizontal bars to indicate seniority. Navy pilots and crew all have marks with wings (qv). The Imperial Japanese Navy, which was closely

modelled on western navies, had a similar range of badges, but with the addition of a traditional chrysanthemum. Intriguingly, medical staff on board Japanese warships wore a red cross.

1

2

3

4

1 British non-substantive insignia for torpedoes; badges with the crown and two stars are no longer in use.

2 Gunner of the Royal Danish Navy.

3 Helmsman of the French Navy.

4 Diver of the German Democratic Navy.

CHEVRONS AND STRIPES

Conventionally, chevrons distinguish the ranks of Lance Corporal, Corporal and Sergeant; however, Colour Sergeants, Master Sergeants and other ranks just below a Warrant Officer can add to the confusion. Chevrons are normally a V-shape, pointing either up or down, and the more stripes, the higher the rank. Some have a letter or design inside the "V" to show the skill or specialization of the NCO. In the US and Danish armed forces the open end of the V may be closed by a curved stripe according to the rank of the NCO. In some armies Warrant Officers display their rank on the cuff. In the US Army the most senior NCO is the Sergeant Major of the Army, who has chevrons which enclose two stars. In the US and Danish navies NCOs wear chevrons rather than cuff bars.

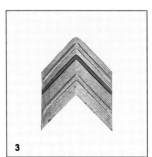

1

2

1 Irish Army Company Sergeant (1963).

2 US Army Sergeant 1st Class.

3 "Caporal-chef" of the French Foreign Legion.

4 US Army Air Force Airman 1st Class.

3

4

BRASSARDS OR ARMLETS

These are normally worn on the right sleeve and can be used to distinguish personnel in civilian clothes, like Civil Defence or the Red Cross, or soldiers with a temporary assignment such as Movements Officers at an airfield or railway station. The United Nations Organisation, with its pale blue armlet and globe insignia, has come increasingly into the public eye. Brassards are armlets with a loop attachment for the shoulder strap. They are often worn by Military Police on duty. The MP brassard, sometimes with a badge above it, can be seen on the sleeves of men or women with their white topped cap, helmet or red beret. Brassards are a good way to display NCO rank and may incorporate a pencil and notebook pocket.

1 Army Medical Services.
2 Transportation Corps, US Marines.
3 One of several variations of the United Nations Forces' armlet.

COMMEMORATIVE INSIGNIA

These can be worn on the breast or shoulder and may record the individual's or his unit's participation in a campaign or action. They are akin to campaign medals (qv). In World War II the Germans instituted medal shields for servicemen involved in major engagements, which began in 1940 with the Narvik, included Krim (Crimea) 1941–1943, Demjansk 1942, Cholm 1942, and ended with Lorient 1944. Warsaw Pact armies wore small enamel badges showing a design and the date of annual military training exercises.

1

2 a

2 b

2 c

1 "Narvik" shield awarded by Germany in World War II.

2 Czechoslovak "joint manoeuvres" badges:

a Shield 1972.   **b** Shield 1984.
c Vltava 1966.

CUFF INSIGNIA

An item of military insignia unique to the German armed forces is displayed on the cuffs of Army and Air Force uniforms. The cuff title, which dates back to before World War I, was greatly expanded in World War II, particularly by divisions of the Waffen-SS. In modified form they are still in use in Germany today. The Leibstandarte SS Adolf Hitler, who originally composed the body guard for the Führer, had a cuff title which bore his signature; others included the French Charlemagne and Norwegian Nordland divisions which served with the Waffen-SS. The Germans also awarded cuff titles as battle honours – the first for Crete and the last for Courland. The Bundeswehr adopted the cuff title after the war for NCO Cadets – Unteroffizierschule and the Wachtbatalion, the Guard

Battalion originally stationed near Bonn. Before World War II all ranks of the Germany Army wore two rectangular patches, in branch-of-service colours on each cuff of the dress tunic.

1 Two cuff patches of the "Nationale Volksarmee" (German Democratic Republic):

a Air Force Officers.

b Artillery, other ranks.

2 Two cuff titles:

a 1st SS Armoured Division "Leibstandarte SS Adolph Hitler".

b 3rd Armoured Division "Totenkopf".

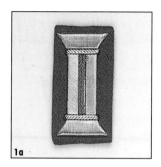

1a

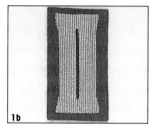

1b

2a

2b

LONG-SERVICE AND OVERSEAS INSIGNIA

Long-service stripes are granted to enlisted men for periods of two or more years of honourable service. They are normally a horizontal bar of coloured tape or woven cloth worn on the cuff, though some armies favour a metal badge worn on the breast. Overseas insignia are also worn on the cuff and were introduced in World War I for a year or six months service. They have been retained in the US Army for World War II, Korea and Vietnam. The Imperial Japanese Navy produced good-conduct chevrons, including one for Excellent Service which had a chrysanthemum in its apex.

1 British overseas service insignia.

2 US Army overseas service insigina.

3 US Army long-service insignia (each stripe represents three years of honourable service).

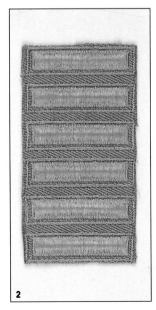

COMBAT BADGES

The German Army in World War II instituted a series of badges for men who had been in action for several days in succession. Some were for Panzer troops, others for infantry, flak gunners, combat and support arms. As the war dragged on men received versions of these badges which showed a total tally of the number of actions in which they had fought. The tank destruction badge, which was worn on the upper

sleeve, was for the single-handed destruction of a tank. A soldier received a gold one for the fifth tank. In the US the Combat Infantryman Badge, or CIB, comes in three forms: a musket with a wreath on an infantry blue background and two other versions with one or two stars. These indicate that the wearer has been awarded the CIB for one, two or three separate armed conflicts – for example World War

II, Korea and Vietnam. A CIB with two stars is known colloquially as a "perfect attendance badge". A Combat Medics Badge was introduced to honour infantry medics, many of whom were killed or wounded in Vietnam rendering first aid.

1 World War II German Tank Battle badge.

2 World War II German General Assault badge.

3 US Combat Infantryman badge.

1

2

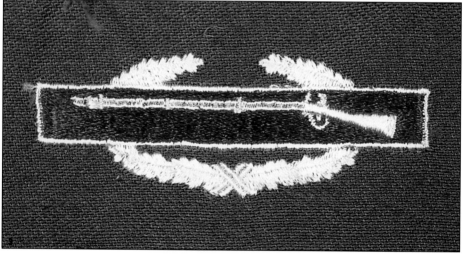

MEDALS AND DECORATIONS

Medals fall loosely into two groups, gallantry and efficiency. Gallantry decorations range from the highest, like the Medal of Honour or Victoria Cross, to that difficult area where men or women have served bravely over a period in the front line, but have not performed a single act of heroism. Efficiency decorations cover both peace and war and may be awarded to men who, while they may not have exhibited heroism, have worked hard and contributed to the success of the armed forces. In the US armed forces some are only ribbons, while others have a medal and ribbon. There is even a miniature of the ribbon for wear with civilian clothes.

1 British 1914–15 Star.

2 Iron Cross Second Class.

3 US Distinguished Service Cross. The Oak Leaves indicate an additional award.

GALLANTRY DECORATIONS

Awards for outstanding bravery, like the US Medal of Honour, the British Victoria Cross, the French Legion of Honour with Croix de Guerre, or the Netherlands Military Order of William, always attract attention, partly because there are so few recipients and they are men or women of unique courage. The Medal of Honour dates back to 1861, when it was instituted for the Navy. It is now awarded in three styles for the US Navy, Army and Air Force. The US Marine Corps receive the US Navy award. All are neck orders hung on a pale blue ribbon with 13 stars.

1 Navy Medal of Honor (1942–Present).

2 Army Medal of Honor (1944–Present).

3 US Air Force Medal of Honor.

CAMPAIGN MEDALS

Like commemorative decorations (qv) and cuff titles (qv), campaign medals record an individual's participation in a battle or campaign. US campaign medals began with the Civil War Medal and Indian Wars medals, which were authorized in 1907. The latest is the medal issued in 1991 to troops who fought in Operation Desert Shield/Storm. A number of expedition medals were awarded between the wars, including the Yangtze Service Medal and the Nicaraguan Campaign Medal. In World War II US servicemen and women could receive the European-African-Middle Eastern Campaign Medal, whereas their British comrades could in theory receive up to four medals – for service in France 1939–40, North Africa, Italy and Northwest Europe.

1 Civil War Medal (Army, with original ribbon).

2 US European-African-Middle Eastern campaign medal.

3 German-Italian African campaign medal.

WOUND STRIPES, BADGES AND MEDALS

Stripes have been awarded to recognize wounds received in action in the British, Belgian, Italian and Red Armies; other armies favour a medal or badge. The German Army in World War I instituted a wound badge, which was expanded in the Spanish Civil War and World War II for the first and subsequent wounds. After the attempt on his life in July 1944, Hitler sanctioned a special wound badge for survivors of the bomb plot which bore the date and his signature. The most famous wound insignia is the US Purple Heart, which was established by George Washington in 1782; a medal was authorized in 1932 and in 1985 it was elevated by President Ronald Reagan to a status just below the Bronze Star.

2

1

1 US Purple Heart.
2 Third Reich Wound Badge.

UNIT CITATIONS AND UNIT AWARDS

Created by President Roosevelt in World War II to honour units which had distinguished themselves in combat, a citation is similar in spirit to the honour of a fourragere (qv), since every man and woman in the unit may wear it. The Presidential Unit Citation for the Army and Air Force is a blue ribbon with a gold metal wreath border; the Marine Corps and Navy have a red, yellow and blue ribbon. Other awards include Meritorious Unit Commendation and the Navy "E" Award Ribbon for efficiency. In uniform, citation and unit awards are worn on the right breast.

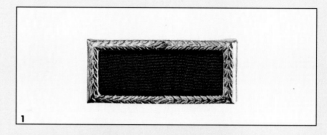

2

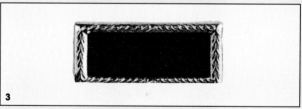

3

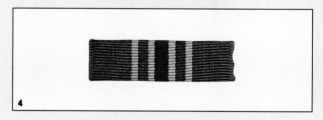

1

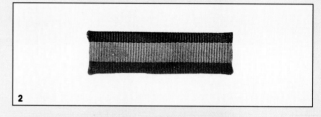

4

5

1 US Presidential Unit Citation (Army and Air Force).

2 US Presidential Unit Citation (Navy and Marine Corps).

3 US Army Meritorious Unit Commendation.

4 US Navy Meritorious Unit Commendation.

5 Navy "E" Award Ribbon.

GOOD CONDUCT MEDAL

While some awards for long service and good conduct may be badges worn on the breast, which is an Eastern European and Russian practice, others are in the form of medals. The US armed forces have a range of good-conduct medals for the Navy, Army, Marine Corps and Air Force. In addition, the Coast Guard and Reserves have their own. One year's creditable service in war or three or four in peacetime qualify a serviceman or woman for these decorations. In 1986 President Ronald Reagan instituted a Prisoner of War Medal, backdated to 1917.

1

2

3

4

1 US Army Good Conduct medal.

2 US Navy Good Conduct medal.

3 US Marine Corps Good Conduct medal.

4 US Air Force Good Conduct medal.

BUTTONS

While some armies, like the German, favour a plain white metal button, stippled so that it does not reflect, others show regimental or national motifs. In the past brass was the most common material for buttons, since it was non-corrosive and smart when polished. War-time restrictions and the wide use of combat clothing in World War II led to the adoption of drab plastic. Modern parade uniforms use buttons with a gilt effect, which saves the serviceman or woman hours of difficult polishing. These gilt buttons are favoured for regimental or service blazers. The smallest buttons are attached to the chin-strap of service dress caps and the largest to greatcoats.

1

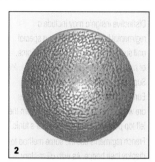

2

3

4

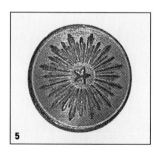

5

6

7

8

1 France.

2 Germany (pre-1945).

3 Republic of Ireland.

4 Spain.

5 Sweden.

6 Poland.

7 USA (for greatcoat).

8 Two British Army buttons.

DISTINCTIVE INSIGNIA

Distinctive insignia may include a regimental badge, a badge for a special unit such as the NATO ACE Mobile Force, or headquarters insignia – for example, for Supreme Headquarters Allied Powers Europe (SHAPE). Many of these badges are worn on a leather fob hanging from the left top pocket button of the soldier's tunic. French regiments use the same method to display their badge. As with all military insignia they draw on classic military

heraldic designs and devices. Distinctive insignia may also be worn as a pin-backed badge on the tunic front or on the shoulder straps of dress uniforms. US Army badges are often ingenious designs which use arm colours as a background – pale blue for infantry, red for artillery and maroon and white for medical corps.

1 Cross of Lorraine of the Free French.

2 French Fascists.

3 8th Marine Infantry Parachute Regiment (France).

1

2

3

NATIONAL INSIGNIA

The German Reichsadler breast eagle and swastika from World War II is one of the most powerful national insignia images. National insignia may also appear as a cap badge. In World War II Allied troops wore a national shoulder title (qv). Where troops are part of an international force they may also have a miniature version of their national flag sewn onto a shoulder of their uniform as a further means of identification. Interestingly, the Germans adopted the same practice with the men they recruited from occupied countries; French Waffen-SS and Wehrmacht troops fighting the Russians had a tricolour shield on the right arm of their uniforms, identical to that worn by French personnel serving with the US Army in Europe. Today US service personnel wear a tape above the left top pocket to identify their arm and their name above the other.

1

2

1 Third Reich "Wehrmacht" breast badge, army officers.

2 Waffen-SS sleeve badge, other ranks.

3 British badge.

4 US Air Force breast insignia.

3

4

POCKET INSIGNIA

In the US armed forces regiments and schools which do not qualify for shoulder insignia wear a patch on the pocket of combat kit or working shirts. Like patches (qv) these were originally in full colour, but are now in subdued black and green.

Among the units with pocket insignia are the Sea Bees – the US Navy Construction Battalions – Missile Wings of the USAF and reconnaissance and special forces units. On flying overalls pocket insignia may reflect the specialized role of a squadron, such as reconnaissance or anti-submarine operations.

1 501st Tactical Missile Wing, a unit of the US Air Force.

2 US Special Forces.

2

BELT BUCKLES

Like the cap badge (qv) the belt buckle is a focus of attention during an inspection. Originally made from brass or white metal, sometimes with a contrasting metal inlay, it could be on white pipe clayed parade belts or black leather load-carrying belts. Buckles often carry national insignia (qv) or corps insignia. German Army belts have featured the motto "Gott Mit Uns" ("God with Us") since before World War I. After the war it was replaced by the motto "Freiheit Einigkeit Recht" ("Freedom the Only Right"). The East German Army (NVA) had a buckle which featured a hammer and dividers within a wreath of corn. Naval ratings of the former Soviet Union wore a black belt with a large brass buckle with an anchor and star with hammer and sickle. In some forces a distinction is made between officers and men. Thus Waffen-SS officers and men may have shared the same motto on their buckles – "Meine Ehre heist Treue" ("My Honour is Loyalty"), but the designs were distinct.

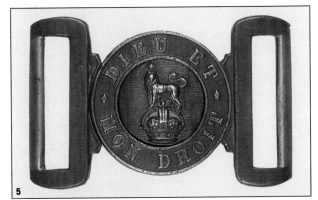

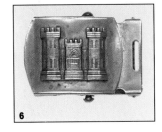

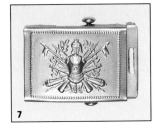

1 Austrian buckle.

2 Victorian buckle of the Royal Engineers.

3 World War I German buckle.

4 Spanish Infantry buckle.

5 Other ranks' universal pattern 1881/1902 of the British Army.

6 US Army buckle (Engineers).

7 Italian Army buckle.

S W O R D S ,   D A G G E R S   A N D   S W O R D   K N O T S

A sword or dagger has long been a symbol of military status. Though Japanese officers and NCOs carried swords in World War II, the practice was discontinued by most armies in World War I. They remain, however, for wear with parade uniforms. The dagger is normally worn by naval officers and the sword by men in the army. The sword knot was originally a loop of leather which secured the sword to the soldier's wrist, so that he could not lose it in action. It is now a symbolic item made from leather or woven aluminium thread and may be attached to a bayonet frog, dagger or sword. In World War I and II the German armed forces produced a complex range of knots identifying rank and arm by designs and colours. With the rise of the Nazis in Germany in the 1930s, swords, daggers and cleavers were given a special place in the uniforms of both military and civil functionaries. Some were practical, but most were to show the status of the officer. Combat knives were widely used by the Allies in World War II, but with the exception of the Fairburn Sykes dagger, they did not appear as military insignia.

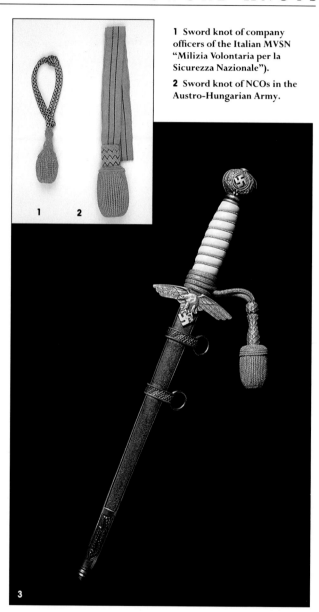

1 Sword knot of company officers of the Italian MVSN "Milizia Volontaria per la Sicurezza Nazionale").

2 Sword knot of NCOs in the Austro-Hungarian Army.

3 A Third Reich "Luftwaffe" dagger of the post-1937 era.

SYMBOLS AND HERALDRY

Most rank insignia or unit patches draw on heraldic or symbolic motifs or designs. Heraldry played an important part in the designs of early medieval uniforms because the colours of a knight usually included his lord's coat of arms. The royal herald, who always accompanied the king in battle, wore an elaborate tabard decorated according to the strict rules of heraldry. Military designs have no such stringency: almost anything that

a regiment or branch of service wishes to use as a symbol may find its way on to a uniform. Weapons and animals are popular, while symbols of force or power like lightning bolts or wings are often incorporated. Some unusual designs have appeared, including a spider proposed for the US Army 135th Airborne Division and a ghost unit devised in World War II. The 81st Infantry Division, with its wild cat, has a provenance dating back to

World War I. The British No. 1 Commando has a salamander engulfed in flames, while the 56th Division has a black cat. The Belgian Chasseurs Ardennaise have a wild boar as a cap badge (qv) and collar dog (qv).

1 81st Infantry Division of US Army patch.

2 56th (London) Armoured Division, 3rd pattern, of the British Army flash.

3 Cap badge of the Belgian Chasseurs Ardennaise.

SWORDS, SABRES AND SCIMITARS

The British Army Physical Training Corps has a cap badge of crossed sabres, which also features as part of NCO rank insignia (qv). In other armies crossed sabres are normally worn by soldiers in cavalry or armoured units. The Australian Army Aviation Corps has an eagle holding crossed swords in its talons The British, Danes, Greeks, Dutch, Norwegians, Spanish and Turkish are among the armed forces that use these motifs. The 13th Waffen-SS Division Kama, composed of Croatian Muslims, had a cap badge with a scimitar. The sword piercing the darkness of Nazi Occupation was the symbol on the badge worn by staff at the Supreme Headquarters Allied Expeditionary Force (SHAEF). During the Vietnam war the 1st Aviation Brigade had a patch with a sword and an eagle, while a sword on a shield was the patch for the Military Assistance Command Vietnam (MACV) and the US Army Vietnam.

1 **British Army Physical Training Corps cap badge.**

2 **Australian Army Aviation Corps cap badge.**

3 **Patch of US Military Assistance Command Vietnam (MACV).**

DAGGERS AND BAYONETS

Probably the most famous cap badge with a sword is that of the SAS, which shows the legendary sword Excalibur, not, as many think, a winged dagger. Men of the British Army who have completed the Commando course which qualifies them to serve with the Royal Marines wear a dagger badge on their service dress and pullovers. In World War II the patch for the US 10th Mountain Division had crossed bayonets and the 63rd Division has a bayonet against a background of flames. The bayonet appears in the patch worn by the post-war 75th Regimental Combat Team and the 1st, 2nd, 171st, 172nd, 173rd, 193rd, 198th and 205th Brigades. In the British army a red bayonet has been adopted as the symbol of the infantry. The US Army Special Forces patch shows a dagger piercing lightning bolts, which earned it the nickname of the "Saigon Electrical Works badge" during the Vietnam War.

1 **Collar insignia of Special Air Service Regiment (SAS) of the British Army.**

2 **US Army Special Forces patch.**

3 **63rd Infantry Division of US Army.**

WREATHS AND OAK LEAVES

Oak or olive wreaths are used as part of the cap badge and rank insignia of many armies. The wreath dates back to the ancient tribute to the victor in battle. Both the West German and former East German Army adopted the oak leaf collar patch (qv) which had been worn by General officers in the Imperial and Nazi German armies. Wreaths feature in the cap badges of the Belgian, British, Danish, French (Navy only), German, Greek, Italian, Luxembourg, Dutch, Norwegian, Portuguese (Navy and Air Force), Spanish and Turkish armed forces. Gold oak leaves are also used on the peaks of senior officer's caps. The US Air Force, however, has silver clouds with lightning bolts.

1 3rd Reich Army officer's badges for the peaked cap.

2 "Nationale Volksarmee" peaked cap badge for generals.

3 Peaked cap badge for officers of "Nationale Volksarmee".

4 Royal Air Force cap badge.

GRENADES

The grenade dates back to the invention of gunpowder, but became significant in the 18th century when the elite "Grenadiers" used it in action. The British Grenadier Guards and Fusiliers continue this tradition. The grenade is also used as a cap badge (qv) by Royal Engineer officers and is the collar dog (qv) of both Engineers and Artillery officers. It is the insignia of the Belgian and French Gendarmerie and the Italian Carabinieri paramilitary forces. The Greek, Italian and French Army have the grenade for cap badge and rank. The French Foreign Legion infantry have a unique seven-flamed grenade as their cap badge.

1 Cap badge for warrant officers, orderly room sergeants and band sergeants of the British Grenadier Guards.

2 Cap badge of the Royal Scots Fusiliers.

3 Collar insignia of Britian's Corps of Royal Engineers.

DEATH'S HEAD

The Death's Head as a cap badge (qv) dates back to the 19th century, when it was worn by Prussian troops. It is the cap badge of the British 17/21 Lancers. Italian Fascist anti-partisan units known as the Black Brigades wore a skull and crossed bones badge. However, it is chiefly associated with the SS

and their brief and sanguinary career in Germany and Occupied Europe from 1933 to 1945. Their insignia featured a special version of the Death's Head as a cap badge (a different version was worn by tank troops of the Germany Army). SS-Division Totenkopf (Death's Head) wore this insignia on their

collars. Collars had the letters SS as a runic version of a double lightning flash. Non-German SS troops were not permitted to wear the SS runes, but did have cuff titles (qv). The SS had its own version of the Reichsadler (eagle) (qv), which was worn on the upper sleeve.

1 Italian Black Brigade badge.

2 "Totenkopf" Division collar patch.

3 Pocket patch of US Armed Forces: 1st Battalion 13th Infantry Regiment Reconnaissance.

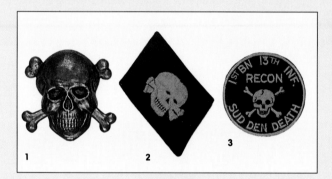

AXES

As a tool or a weapon the axe features in many ways. French Foreign Legion Pioneers carry axes on parade – and they are all the more striking for having beards and wearing leather aprons. British infantry pioneer sergeants, also permitted to have beards, assault pioneers and the Royal Pioneer Corps have axes in their insignia and cap badge. On parades the Household Cavalry includes a farrier who carries a symbolic axe. In World War II pontoon troops in the Belgian army had crossed-axes insignia. Italian sappers, signals, railway engineers and miners all had crossed axes against a grenade (qv) cap badge (qv). The elegant pre-war enamel badges for Polish engineer troops had picks, shovels and axes. The patches for US Army 65th, 70th and 84th Divisions all feature axes, while that for the 19th Corps showed an Indian tomahawk. The current Norwegian army has a lion holding a Norseman's axe in its claws.

1 The white tomahawk of the US Army's 19th Corps.

2 Collar patch and badge of Sweden's Engineers, worn on the service dress jacket.

3 Italian black brigade badge showing fasces (bundles of rods and axe head).

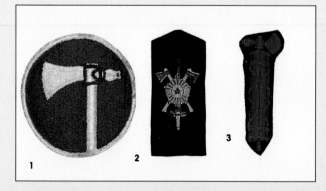

EAGLES AND WINGS

The Austrian Army has a version of the old Imperial Austro-Hungarian eagle. The Polish armed forces feature both the eagle and symbolic wings. Senior officers in the Italian Army have the eagle as a cap badge and officers as do senior NCOs in the Italian Air Force. The Dutch Air Force has an eagle which looks very similar to the British RAF bird. The Norwegian Air Force has a diving eagle in a wreath, a little like the British Army Air Corps badge. The Portuguese Air Force has an eagle in flight within a wreath and the Spanish Army has the national symbol as a cap badge. The Turkish Air Force has an eagle surmounting a crescent within a wreath. The British Royal Air Force has an eagle as a service dress cap badge. The US Navy, Army and Air Force all have variants of the US bald eagle as cap badges, as well as rank insignia, and full Colonel has it as rank (qv) insignia, earning the title "Bird Colonel". The 101st Airborne Division has its famous screaming eagle on a black shield-shaped patch. The Royal Scots Greys, which was merged with the Royal Scots Dragoon Guards, has as a cap badge the French Imperial Eagle, which the regiment captured at Waterloo in 1815.

1 Post-1955 Austrian double-headed eagle for the peaked cap.

2 Royal Air Force badge for officer's peaked cap.

3 Patch for the 101st Infantry Division of the US Army, which became Airborne in 1943.

WINGS AND CLAWS

The Danish Air Force has a winged Royal shield. French paratroops have a cap badge (qv) showing a winged eagle's claw grasping a dagger (qv), while the French Air Force has a red wing motif for its cap badge. War-time and post-war German Air Force collar patch (qv) rank insignia combined a wing motif embroidered in grey cotton or aluminium thread against an arm colour. US Army Pathfinders have a badge showing a winged torch lighting the way. The war-time 17th Airborne Division had a yellow claw against a black background. HQ staff in the 1st Allied Airborne Army had a patch with a winged "1".

1 Beret badge of French Parachutists

2 Patch for the 17th Airborne Division of the US Army.

3 US Army Pathfinders badge.

LIONS

Just as the eagle has a reputation for strength and power so too does the lion. The lion appears on the Belgian Air Force and Medical Service cap badge (qv) and the Danish Army has the Royal crest with three lions. The Luxembourg Army, a battalion-size force, has a lion within a shield. The Netherlands Army has a lion within a circular badge. In the British army officers above the rank of Colonel have a Royal lion surmounting their cap badge. Until they became part of the Adjutant General's Corps, the British Womens Royal Army Corps (WRAC) wore their own cap badge, which featured a lioness.

1 Lion cap badge used by Belgian troops in Britain.

2 Post World War II Danish beret badge.

3 Embroidered cap badge of British army general for the peaked cap.

4 The King's Own Royal Regiment (Lancaster) cap badge.

4

CROWNS

Where a monarch is the head of state – Norway, Denmark, Luxembourg, Belgium, Holland, Spain and Great Britain as well as some countries in the Middle East and Far East – the crown is a useful item of military insignia. It is used either as a cap badge or as a rank insignia to mark the status of an officer as holding field rank – major and above. For NCOs its incorporation in rank insignia shows that the NCO is a Colour sergeant or above. In Operation Desert Shield/Storm US officers wore Saudi rank, which is similar to British, on a pocket fob. Some Saudi officers wore a fob with their equivalent US rank.

1 Belgian crown.

2 Danish crown.

3 Lieutenant Colonel of the British Army.

4 Colonel of the British army (plastic).

DRAGONS

Welsh regiments in the British army use the dragon as insignia – which was also an element of the national insignia (qv). The World War II Wessex Brigade wore a Wyverne (a type of dragon) and after the war this was used as the cap badge of the Territorial Army Wessex Regiment. The Royal Army Dental

Corps had a dragon grasping a sword (qv) in its jaws. The Buffs and Royal Berkshire Regiment, two infantry regiments which fought in China in the 19th century, had a dragon cap badge (qv). The patch for the World War II US 18th Airborne Corps and the 13th Airborne Division both featured a dragon.

1 Cap badge of The Buffs (Royal East Kent Regiment) (British Army).

2 Cap badge of the Royal Army Dental Corps.

3 18th Corps of the US Army (made Airborne in 1944).

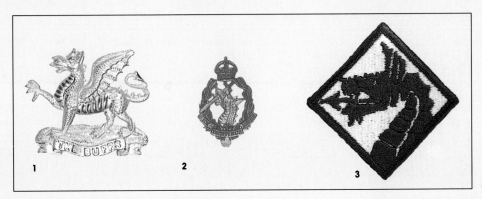

ANCHORS

The anchor is almost universal as the insignia for naval forces – exceptions are Canada and Belgium. In the German Navy in World War II elegant trade badges featured an anchor as the background to devices like crossed cannon for a gunnery artificer or a steering wheel for a driver. US Navy petty officers have an anchor cap badge which includes stars and other devices to show their rank. Spanish Marines and Navy have anchors as cap badges (qv), though the designs are different. Incidentally, the US Marines Corps and British Royal Marines both have a cap badge showing the globe – the USMC shows the western hemisphere and the RM the eastern. In World War II both the British and US forces adopted a cloth badge showing an eagle (qv), anchor and Thompson sub-machine gun for combined operations or amphibious units. This badge, in a modified form, appeared on the British medal issued to troops who fought in the Gulf War.

1 US Marine Corps officer's cap badge.

2 Royal Navy "foul anchor".

3 Soviet Navy petty officer's cap badge.

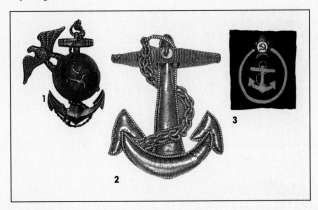

INDEX

· · · · · · ·

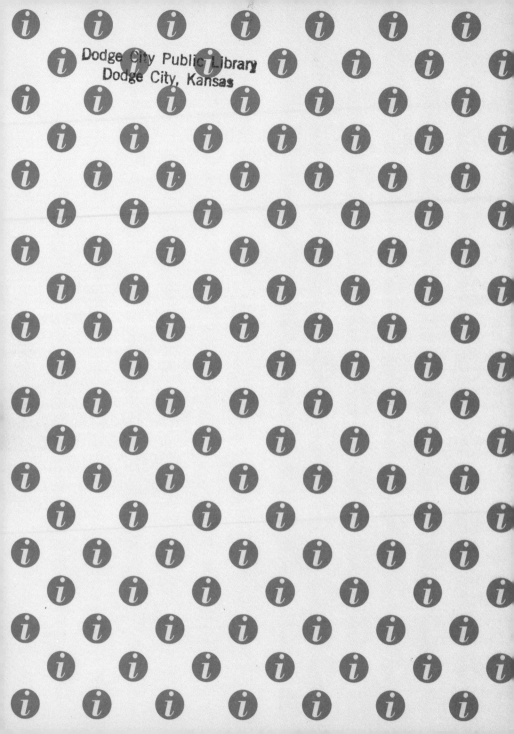